Penis

A COMPREHENSIVE GUIDEBOOK FOR MEN WITH TINY DICKS TO OVERCOME STIGMA, EXPLORE SEXUAL FANTASIES AND TO FIND THE RIGHT SUPPORT SYSTEM

By

GARCIA SCOTT FRAZIER

© Copy right 2023

Table of Contents

Introduction 4

Chapter 1 16

  Accepting Your Reality 16

Chapter 2 19

  Understanding the Anatomy of the Penis . 19

  Is the Size of Penis Hereditary? 22

  Other factors that can affect the size of your penis 24

Chapter 3 27

  The Psychological Impact of Having a Small Penis 27

Chapter 4 30

  Exploring Alternative Sexual Techniques .. 30

Chapter 5 34

  Understanding the Role of Penis Pumps and Other Devices 34

  How may penis enlargement surgery be beneficial? 36

Chapter 6 39

  Seeking Professional Help 39

Chapter 7 42
  Embracing Your Unique Qualities..................42
Chapter 9 45
  Communicating with Your Partner...............45
Chapter 10..48
  Understanding the Connection between Confidence and Sexual Performance..........48
Chapter 11..51
  Overcoming the Stigma of Having a Small Penis..51
Chapter 12..53
  Exploring Sexual Fantasies and Role-playing...53
Chapter 13..56
  Finding the Right Support System. 56
Conclusion..59

Introduction

For many men, having a small penis can be a stressful and challenging experience. It may result in worry, low self-esteem, and feelings of insecurity. There are numerous methods to deal with the difficulties of having a little penis, but it's vital to keep in mind that your size does not determine who you are as a person. You can learn to have a happy and fulfilled life by comprehending the anatomy of the penis, investigating alternative sexual practices, getting professional advice, and accepting your individual characteristics. You can overcome the difficulties of having a small penis with the appropriate attitude and support, and you can learn to accept and love yourself for who you are.

The several facets of having a small penis will be covered in this article, along with helpful advice and techniques to assist you get through the difficulties. We'll talk about the psychological effects of having a tiny penis and look at various strategies for enhancing confidence and self-worth. We will also go over the function of penile pumps and other gadgets, as well as why it's critical to seek professional assistance if you are suffering psychological difficulties as a result of having a small penis. We'll also talk about the value of communicating with your partner and how to get over the stigma associated with having a small penis. With the help of this manual, you will discover how to live with a little penis and how to have satisfying sex.

What are the reasons behind some women's preference for smaller penises?

Many believe that a larger penis is preferable due to societal pressures. However, this is not necessarily true for all women. There are many reasons why some women may prefer smaller penises.

First and foremost, it is important to understand that sexual pleasure and satisfaction are not solely determined by the size of the penis. Research has shown that clitoral stimulation, rather than vaginal penetration, is the primary method used by women to achieve orgasm. Therefore, a smaller penis may not necessarily hinder sexual enjoyment.

In fact, some studies have suggested that a smaller penis can actually make some women feel more comfortable during sex. A larger penis may cause discomfort or pain for both partners, which could negatively impact the sexual experience. With a smaller penis, these issues may not occur as frequently.

Personal preference is another potential explanation for why some women may prefer smaller penises. Just as some men may prefer certain physical attributes in a partner, such as larger breasts or a curvier physique, some women may prefer a smaller penis.

Psychological factors may also play a role in why some women prefer smaller penises. A smaller penis may be associated with a partner or themselves feeling vulnerable, which can be appealing. This may be tied to cultural and societal pressures that often reinforce the idea that men should be dominant and in control.

Individual experiences may also shape a woman's preferences for penis size. If a woman has had positive sexual experiences with men who had smaller penises in the past, this may influence her preferences going forward.

It's important to remember that every woman is unique and may have her own reasons for preferring a smaller penis. Ultimately, it's crucial to understand that penis size is not the only factor that affects sexual satisfaction or pleasure. Communication and intimacy are key components of a fulfilling sexual experience.

What factors are responsible for determining the size of the penis?

For a long time, the size of a man's penis has been a topic of conversation and discussion. Many men are interested in learning about what factors can affect the size of their penis and whether it's possible to make it bigger. This article will explore the various factors that influence penis size and discuss ways to improve it.

Genetics is the most critical and primary factor that determines penis size. Hormonal levels and genetic makeup play a role in shaping the size and structure of the penis. Studies suggest that heredity accounts for approximately 60-85% of the penis's size, indicating that genes play a significant role in determining penis size.

Environmental aspects like nutrition, physical health, and chemical exposure can also influence penis size. During puberty, a diet that is high in protein and low in fat may aid in growth, while herbicides and heavy metals may impede growth.

Hormones are also a crucial factor in penis size. Testosterone is the main hormone responsible for penis growth and development. Low testosterone levels can result in a smaller penis.

Age is another determining factor that affects penis size. The penis develops rapidly during adolescence and reaches its maximum size by the age of 18.

After that, the penis will not grow any more significant.

Finally, lifestyle habits like smoking and excessive alcohol consumption can influence penis size. These behaviors can cause poor blood flow and impair penile growth.

There are various options available for men who are concerned about their penis size. Although penis enlargement surgery and pumps are popular options, they may have adverse side effects and risks. Instead, leading a healthy lifestyle that includes a well-balanced diet, regular exercise, and avoiding tobacco and excessive alcohol consumption can improve overall well-being and sexual health.

Is it a good idea to have penis enlargement surgery?

Determining whether or not penis enlargement surgery is worth the investment is a complex matter that requires a thorough understanding of the various factors involved. One of the key things to keep in mind is that penis size is not the sole determinant of sexual pleasure or satisfaction. Other factors, such as communication, technique, and emotional connection, also play an important role in overall sexual satisfaction.

Additionally, it is crucial to note that there is no one-size-fits-all solution when it comes to penis enlargement surgery. There are numerous different types of surgeries that each come with their own set of pros and cons. For example, some surgeries utilize silicone injections, while others involve cutting and stretching the penis. However, each of these procedures carries risks such as scarring, infection, and loss of sensitivity.

Cost is another major factor that should be considered before deciding to undergo penis enlargement surgery. The procedure can be quite expensive, and most insurance plans do not cover the cost. Additionally, there is no guarantee that the surgery will be successful, and there is always a risk of complications.

Ultimately, the decision to pursue surgery to increase penis size is a highly personal one that should be made with careful consideration of all the potential risks and benefits. Before making a decision, it is important to consult with a qualified healthcare provider and conduct thorough research on the available options. If surgery is chosen, it is essential to select a reputable surgeon and closely follow all post-operative instructions to achieve the best possible outcome.

Chapter 1
Accepting Your Reality

The first and most crucial step in adjusting to having a small penis is accepting your situation as it is. It can be challenging to accept that your penis is smaller than average, but it's vital to keep in mind that your physical characteristics are not determined by its size. You should put more emphasis on your positive traits and qualities because your worth and value as a person are not based on the size of your penis. It's critical to realize that having a small penis is not a disease that can be "fixed" or "cured," nor is it something that can be "corrected." Similar to variances in height, hair color, or eye color, it is merely a variety in size. It's crucial to keep in mind that having a little penis does not denote weakness or inferiority and does not lessen your status as a man.

It's also essential to recognize the successful and joyful sex lives of many men who have small penises. There are many other ways to make your partner and yourself happy outside size, which is not the sole determinant in sexual enjoyment. You can still have a fulfilling and happy sex life by concentrating on other facets of your sexual performance, such as foreplay, communication, and experimenting with various sexual positions.

When embracing your reality, it's essential to have reasonable expectations. It's crucial to avoid making comparisons to other people and to avoid using arbitrary benchmarks like pornography as a guide. It's crucial to keep in mind that acceptance is a process and that accepting the truth about your little penis takes time. It's crucial to have patience with oneself and to keep in mind that having conflicting emotions is common.

Finally, if you are having trouble accepting reality, it's critical to get assistance and help. There are various tools you can use to accept your reality and move forward in a healthy way, including support groups, therapists, and counselors. These resources can assist you in working through your feelings. Keep in mind that you are not alone and that a brighter tomorrow is always possible.

Chapter 2
Understanding the Anatomy of the Penis

Knowing the structure of the penis is essential to comprehending why you have a tiny penis. The shaft, glans, and foreskin are the three primary components of the penis. The shaft's length and the glans' dimensions both determine the penis' size.

The shaft, which is the primary component of the penis, determines how long it is. The corpora cavernosa and the corpus spongiosum are two of the three cylindrical erectile tissue bodies that make up this structure. The primary blood arteries that produce an erection by supplying blood to the penis are called corpora cavernosa.

The glans, which is the penis' head, determines the size of the penis. The foreskin covers the corpus spongiosum, a delicate tissue that makes up the organ. The amount of blood flow that the glans receives during an erection determines the size of the glans.

The skin that encircles the penis's head is known as the foreskin. Circumcision can be used to get rid of it because it is not required for sexual pleasure. The foreskin has no impact on penis size.

It's essential to keep in mind that other factors, besides penis size, affect sexual enjoyment. Many guys who have tiny penises had successful and satisfying sexual lives. Foreplay, communicating, and experimenting with different sexual positions are just a few other methods to make both your partner and yourself happy. It's also crucial to keep in mind that the size of the penis can change significantly based on factors like age, temperature, and sexual excitement, making it a poor indicator of the potential for sexual pleasure.

It's crucial to realize that there is a wide range of what is "normal" in terms of penis size and that different people may have different ideas of what constitutes a tiny penis. Although this is not a precise measurement and can vary widely based on various factors, the average penis size when erect is roughly 5.16 inches (13.12 cm) long and 4.59 inches (11.66 cm) in circumference.

Is the Size of Penis Hereditary?

Many men may ponder whether the size of their penis is genetically predetermined or whether it may be increased using a variety of techniques. The genetic nature of penis size is one of the most often asked questions.

Yes, in a nutshell, one's parents can contribute to the size of their penis. Hormone concentrations and genetic makeup influence the size and form of the penis. According to research, 60–85% of the size of the penis can be attributed to heredity, which means that genetics have a big impact on penile size.

It's important to remember that there are other factors besides genetics that affect penis size. The environment can also affect how the penis develops, including nutrition, health, and exposure to specific substances.

The fact that there is a wide range of normal when it comes to penis size is also important to note. The size of the average penis when erect is around 5.16 inches, according to a study published in the British Journal of Urology International. A penis size of 4 inches or less while erect is still regarded as normal, despite the fact that this measurement might vary substantially.

Consequently, although genetics certainly influence penis size, it is not the primary cause. Furthermore, it's crucial to keep in mind that there is a large range of typical penis sizes and that penis size is not a reliable indicator of sexual satisfaction or pleasure.

Therefore, it can be said that a person's penis size is heritable and that this heritability ranges from 60 to 85%. The penis, however, can also be influenced by environmental factors like nutrition, health, and exposure to specific toxins. Furthermore, it's crucial to keep in mind that there is a large range of typical penis sizes and that penis size is not a reliable indicator of sexual satisfaction or pleasure.

Other factors that can affect the size of your penis
The size of your penis may also be affected by your overall health and specific medical conditions. Obesity, for example, is a major factor, as excess fat around the base of the penis may make it

appear smaller. Weight loss through a healthy diet and exercise can help reduce this fat and increase penis size. Specific medical conditions such as Peyronie's disease can cause the penis to bend or curve due to scar tissue formation, leading to discomfort during erections and potentially a smaller penis. Medications, including antidepressants and blood pressure medications, may also decrease blood flow to the penis, causing it to appear smaller. Poor circulation resulting from smoking, high blood pressure, and other medical conditions can also affect penis size. Increasing circulation through regular exercise, quitting smoking, and treating underlying medical conditions may lead to an increase in penis size. Psychological factors, such as low self-esteem, anxiety, or depression, can also play a role. Men who feel insecure or inadequate about the size of their penis due to negative self-perception may benefit from counseling or therapy to address these feelings and boost their overall self-esteem.

Chapter 3
The Psychological Impact of Having a Small Penis

Many men may experience major psychological effects as a result of having a tiny penis. It may result in worry, low self-esteem, and feelings of insecurity. It's crucial to keep in mind that you are not alone in experiencing these emotions because they are normal.

Men may experience self-consciousness and lose confidence in their ability to satisfy their spouse in bed if they have a small penis. Additionally, it could make them feel inferior and less like a guy. These emotions can cause anxiety and despair and negatively affect their general well-being.

It's also essential to remember that a man's small penis does not automatically denote a lack of masculinity or manliness. It's essential to distinguish between one's penis size and masculinity. It's crucial to realize that there are numerous other ways to make your partner and yourself happy, including foreplay, communication, and experimenting with various sexual positions. Sexual enjoyment is not solely dependent on size.

Additionally, it's critical to acknowledge the happy and fulfilling sex lives of many guys who have small penises. It's critical to keep in mind that there are a variety of enjoyable and interesting aspects of sexual performance, and that sexual pleasure is not solely based on penis size.

It's important to get professional assistance if you're having trouble dealing with the psychological effects of having a small penis. A therapist or counselor may assist you in processing your emotions and provide you tips on how to boost your confidence and self-esteem. They can also teach you methods for overcoming despair and anxiety.

An excellent method to connect with other men who are going through comparable circumstances is by joining a support group. They may be a tremendous source of support and encouragement as well as a sense of community and understanding.

Chapter 4
Exploring Alternative Sexual Techniques

The first step in figuring out how to live with a little penis is to investigate alternative sexual practices. The mere fact that your penis is little does not preclude you from engaging in pleasant sex. You might try a variety of alternate sexual strategies to make up for your little penis.

During sexual contact, concentrating on activating your partner's clitoris or G-spot can help you experience more sexual pleasure. Using a vibrator or direct touch to stimulate the clitoris, a very sensitive organ, is possible. A "come here" gesture with the finger or a specially made toy can be used to stimulate the G-spot, a sensitive location inside the vagina.

Experimenting with various postures is another approach to learn about alternative sexual techniques. Men with small penises could feel more at ease in certain postures, including the doggy position. These postures can also offer deeper penetration and raise the likelihood that the G-spot will be touched. The woman may also be able to control the depth and angle of penetration in some positions, such as the cowgirl, which may be more comfortable for men with smaller penises.

Another option for making your lover feel good is through oral sex. In addition to using their hands to stimulate the clitoris or G-spot, men with small penises can concentrate on having oral intercourse with their partners.

Communication is also vital while investigating alternative sexual approaches. It's essential to be open with your spouse about what works and what doesn't, and to be willing to try new ideas. Practicing different techniques and postures can assist yourself and your partner uncover new ways to please each other while also strengthening your sexual bond.

It's essential to remember that sexual enjoyment isn't solely driven by penis size, and that there are numerous other methods to have a successful sex life. With the correct mindset and understanding, you can explore other sexual approaches and find ways to compensate for your little penis while still having enjoyable sex.

Chapter 5
Understanding the Role of Penis Pumps and Other Devices

Penis pumps as well as other devices can be employed to temporarily expand the penis. However, it is essential to understand that such gadgets are not a long-term solution and should be utilized with caution.

Penis pumps work by producing a vacuum surrounding the penis, causing blood to be pumped into the shaft and causing it to erect. This can temporarily increase the length of the penis, but the impact is transient, and the length of the penis will be back to normal once the pump is withdrawn.

The penis is also stretched over time by wearing additional accessories like extenders, weights, and hangers. However, if used improperly or if left on for an extended period of time, these devices may harm or injure the penis. These tools may not function for everyone, and their results are not guaranteed.

Prior to employing these gadgets, it is also crucial to seek medical advice. A doctor or urologist can provide you advice on the efficacy and safety of these devices as well as assist you in deciding whether they are suitable for you.

It's essential to realize that these tools are not a replacement for expert advice or therapy. It's important to get professional assistance if you're having trouble dealing with the psychological effects of having a small penis. A therapist or counselor may assist you in processing your emotions and give you tips on how to boost your confidence and self-esteem.

How may penis enlargement surgery be beneficial?

The goal of penis enlargement surgery, commonly referred to as penile lengthening or widening surgery, is to enlarge the penis. The purpose of the operation is to increase sexual satisfaction and self-confidence while also enhancing the penis' appearance and functionality.

In penile enlargement surgery, a number of various techniques are used, each with their own advantages and disadvantages. Cutting and extending the penis, silicone injections, and tissue grafts are a few frequent procedures.

The size of the penis is increased, which is one of the main advantages of the procedure. This can assist boost sexual gratification and self-confidence while also enhancing penile aesthetics. The capacity to develop and maintain an erection is one sexual function that penis enlargement surgery may occasionally assist to improve.

Moreover, Peyronie's disease and other penile-related anomalies, such as deformities, can be treated by penis augmentation surgery. This can help to enhance the penis's appearance and functionality as well as sexual health and wellbeing in general.

It's crucial to note that penile enlargement surgery has hazards as well. Infection, scars, loss of sensitivity, and unhappiness with the outcomes are a few of the frequent hazards connected to penis enlargement surgery.

Before having penis enlargement surgery, it's vital to examine the risks and advantages with your doctor to see if it's the best option for you. To assist assure the greatest results, it's crucial to select a qualified surgeon with experience doing penile enlargement surgery.

Chapter 6
Seeking Professional Help

It's important to get professional assistance if you have a small penis. It's also important to get professional assistance if you're having trouble dealing with the psychological effects of having a small penis. A therapist or counselor may assist you in processing your emotions and provide you tips on how to boost your confidence and self-esteem.

You can learn coping skills from a therapist to help you deal with the unfavorable thoughts and emotions connected to having a small penis as well as the causes of your sentiments. They can also teach you methods for overcoming despair and anxiety. They can also assist you in exploring your relationship with your body and in appreciating and accepting the special traits that make you who you are.

A professional's assistance should also be sought if you are having problems with your sexuality or have worries about how your sexual organs are functioning. A therapist or counselor may assist you in exploring these issues and can give you tips on how to enhance your sexual performance. Additionally, they may aid in your exploration of alternative sexual practices and the search for solutions to your little penis so that you can still have enjoyable sex.

A medical professional who focuses on the male reproductive system and urinary tract is known as a urologist. You may get their advice on the usefulness and safety of tools like penile pumps as well as how they can help you comprehend the anatomy of the penis.

Furthermore, if required, they can assist you in researching medical choices, including surgery.

Keep in mind that asking for expert assistance does not indicate weakness. It's a brave move toward one's own development and a brighter future. You should be willing to discuss your thoughts and worries with your therapist or counselor and should be open and honest with them. You may learn to embrace and value who you are and live a happy and meaningful life with the correct guidance and support.

Chapter 7
Embracing Your Unique Qualities

A big aspect of coping with a tiny penis is accepting your unique qualities. You can learn to value and embrace yourself for who you are by realizing that there are many other qualities of you that are special and one-of-a-kind.

By recognizing and concentrating on your strengths, you can embrace your individual qualities. Whether it be in the areas of the arts, sports, or intellect, everyone has different strengths and talents. You can develop a sense of appreciation for who you are as a person and the knowledge that you have something unique to contribute to the world by concentrating on your strengths and talents.

Investigating and going after your interests and passions is another way to embrace your distinctive qualities. You can learn to appreciate who you are and find meaning and fulfillment by exploring and pursuing your interests and passions, whether they are hobbies, sports, or creative pursuits.

It's crucial to embrace your individuality by coming to terms with and appreciating your flaws. It's critical to realize that nobody is perfect and that everyone has flaws. You can learn to be kind and compassionate toward yourself and not be too harsh on yourself by accepting and appreciating your flaws.

Additionally, appreciating your distinctive attributes implies accepting yourself exactly as you are; it's important to keep in mind that you are much more than simply your physical attributes and that your value as a person is not based on the size of your penis.

Finally, it's essential to surround oneself with uplifting individuals who will support and motivate you. Your support network may encourage you to recognize the best in yourself and serve as a constant reminder of your value and worth.

Chapter 9
Communicating with Your Partner

Living with a little penis requires you to communicate with your lover on a regular basis. You can increase closeness and trust in your relationship as well as the quality of your sexual encounters by being open and honest with your partner.

Your thoughts and worries regarding your little penis should be one of the most crucial things you discuss with your partner. Your spouse can help you work through any insecurities or anxieties you may be experiencing by having an honest and open conversation with you. You might feel more at ease in your relationship by receiving support and understanding from your partner.

It's important to discuss your sexual needs and aspirations with your spouse. You can try new sexual stances and tactics that can help to compensate for your little penis while still having enjoyable sex by being upfront and honest with your partner. It's also crucial to let your partner know about any sexual troubles you might be having. You may work together to identify answers and enhance your sexual experiences by being open and honest with your partner.

When considering alternate sexual methods, communication is also crucial. You can try various tactics and positions that can help to make up for your little penis and still have happy sex by being upfront and honest with your spouse.

t's also crucial to let your partner know about any medical or therapeutic choices you might be thinking about, such as surgery or the usage of penile pumps or other devices. Together, you can decide what is best for your health and well-being by having an honest and open discussion about it.

Chapter 10
Understanding the Connection between Confidence and Sexual Performance

When you have a small penis, you'll experience several challenges, including understanding the link between self-assurance and sexual performance. A person's ability to perform sexually and their capacity to enjoy the experience are both influenced by their level of confidence, which has a substantial impact on both.

A person's sexual performance can be significantly influenced by their level of body and sexual confidence. A person is more likely to feel relaxed and at ease during sexual activity when they are confidence in their bodies and their sexual prowess, which can result in better sexual performance and a more pleasurable encounter. Contrarily, when a person lacks confidence in their physical appearance or sexual prowess, they may feel anxious or insecure, which can have a detrimental effect on their sexual performance and satisfaction.

The insecurity and anxiety that come with having a small penis can have an impact on a person's confidence in their body and sexual prowess. These uneasy feelings can make it difficult to get and keep an erection, and they can also make it difficult for a person to enjoy and engage in sexual activity.

It's critical to realize that developing confidence is a gradual process that can be aided by a variety of strategies, including therapy, self-help methods, and encouraging self-talk. A person can increase the quality and pleasure of their sexual encounters by concentrating on developing their confidence.

Furthermore, it's critical to keep in mind that confidence involves more than simply one's appearance; it also entails knowing and appreciating one's individual characteristics as well as focusing on one's abilities and skills.

Chapter 11
Overcoming the Stigma of Having a Small Penis

Living with a small penis involves several challenges, one of which is overcoming the stigma associated with it. The social stigma of having a tiny penis is frequently linked to inferiority, inadequacy, and embarrassment. The size of your penis does not, however, define you as a person, so it is crucial to realize that these notions are not grounded in reality.

By becoming knowledgeable about the facts and realities of penis size, you can help yourself overcome the stigma associated with having a tiny penis. You can learn to value and accept your distinctive qualities by realizing that the average penis is significantly smaller than what is frequently shown in the media and that size is not the primary determinant in sexual enjoyment.

Becoming honest and truthful with your spouse is one more approach to get over the stigma associated with having a tiny penis. Building closeness and trust in your relationship, as well as improving your sexual experiences, may be accomplished by being open and honest with your spouse about your thoughts, feelings, and worries.

Chapter 12
Exploring Sexual Fantasies and Role-playing

It is possible to get beyond the limits of having a little penis and still have great sex by exploring sexual fantasies and role-playing. You may discover new methods to please yourself and your partner as well as enhance your performance and satisfaction by playing with various sexual situations and positions.

Sexual fantasies are imaginary pictures or ideas that may be utilized to spark the imagination and spice up a sexual encounter. These fantasies may be personalized to your liking and might contain a variety of settings.

You can discover novel methods to please yourself and your partner as well as enhance your sexual performance and pleasure by exploring your sexual fantasies.

Role-playing is a type of sexual fantasy in which participants act out various roles or scenarios while engaging in sexual activity.

This may apply to situations like a doctor and patient or a master and slave. Role-playing can help you overcome the restrictions of having a tiny penis as well as provide excitement and diversity to your sexual encounters.

When exploring sexual fantasies and role-playing, it's crucial to be open and honest with your partner. You may explore many scenarios and roles that are comfortable for both of you and satisfy both of your wants and desires by being open and honest with your partner.

Furthermore, it's crucial to keep in mind that exploring sexual fantasies and role-playing should be safe and consensual.

Setting limits and ensuring that all parties are at ease with the situation and role-playing are crucial.

.

Chapter 13
Finding the Right Support System.

Living with a tiny penis involves several challenges, including finding the correct support network. Having a support system can help you overcome the difficulties that come with having a tiny penis by offering you emotional, mental, and practical assistance.

Speaking with friends and relatives is one method of locating the ideal support network. You can get emotional support from friends and family, as well as knowledge that you are not alone in your challenges. Additionally, they can assist you in finding materials or conducting research.

Joining online forums or communities is another approach to discover the perfect support network. People who are struggling with comparable challenges might gather in online forums and support groups where they can share their experiences and offer assistance to one another. You can find emotional support, useful guidance, and a feeling of community in these groups. If you are having trouble dealing with the psychological effects of having a tiny penis, you should seek professional assistance.

A therapist or counselor may assist you in processing your emotions and provide you tips on how to boost your confidence and self-esteem.

A fantastic strategy to locate the perfect support system is to find a partner who accepts you for who you are and is prepared to work with you to overcome the difficulties of having a tiny penis. You may work together to discover solutions to make up for your little penis and still have fulfilling sex by being upfront and honest with your spouse.

Conclusion

It can be difficult to live with a little penis, but it's crucial to understand that your size does not define who you are. You can learn to lead a happy and fulfilled life by accepting and loving yourself for who you are and by emphasizing your positive qualities.

Made in the USA
Coppell, TX
23 October 2023